THE LINDA NEMEC FOSTER
FIRST BOOK AWARD FOR POETRY

Under the Honey Locusts

A collection of thresholds and rooms, these are poems made of landscapes and objects and longings that seem to shimmer even in the half-lit house of grief. Here, love is both ghost and guide, a presence that companions even as it fades. Every place we enter feels charged and changed, haunted and blessed by the vision and care of such a poet. The world needs its true artists; Kakie Pate is one of them.

—ALLISON SEAY
author of *To See the Queen*

In a time when many poems adopt the tonal equivalent of clamor in an effort to be heard, along comes Kakie Pate's *Under the Honey Locusts*, a first book of understated lyrics that belie the urgency of their rich emotional depths. "When I got sick," the poet reflects, "I went to the cabin and did not speak / to anyone but the deer." Such vibrant, vital, and admirable reticence enables Pate to genuinely bear witness both to ordinary wonders and profound loss without affectation and with a vividly moving clarity. At once painfully tuned to our "unbelonging" and mindful that "when the sun sets, / the light still remains, victorious," her poems read like messages etched in bark, so finely crafted they appear indelible having become part of the living tree.

—DANIEL TOBIN
author of *Dusk, Empire: New and Selected Poems 1987–2024*

Under
the Honey
Locusts

poems

Kakie Pate

CORNERSTONE PRESS
UNIVERSITY OF WISCONSIN-STEVENS POINT

Cornerstone Press, Stevens Point, Wisconsin 54481
Copyright © 2026 Kakie Pate
www.uwsp.edu/cornerstone

Printed in the United States of America.

Library of Congress Control Number: 2026931035
ISBN: 978-1-968148-45-4

Cover art by Christa MacDonald.

The Linda Nemec Foster First Book Award for Poetry is made possible by the generous support of Linda Nemec and Dr. Tony Foster.

Cornerstone Press titles are produced in courses and internships offered by the Department of English at the University of Wisconsin–Stevens Point.

DIRECTOR & PUBLISHER
Dr. Ross K. Tangedal

EXECUTIVE EDITORS
Jeff Snowbarger, Freesia McKee

EDITORIAL DIRECTOR
Brett Hill

SENIOR EDITORS
Paige Biever

PRESS STAFF
Karlie Harpold, Brianna Loving, Sophie Parish, Oliver McKnight, Sophie McPherson, Sam Bjork, Madison Schultz, Autumn Vine

For Annie and my own future daughter:
May you both see beauty and light fearlessly and often.

CONTENTS

AUTUMN

WINTER

SPRING

SUMMER

AUTUMN

Season of Waiting

After I left you, I took up smoking. Dart
after dart hit pine below the bullseye, forming holes
in the wood that corked the hole in me. Tonight,
I pour myself a glass of wine, and go to sleep.
I play in my dreams—your arms pull at my hips
from behind. Tomorrow morning, I will wake
and you will be gone. The day will be spent wishing
I had picked up a dart in the dark. When I got sick,
I went to the cabin and did not speak
to anyone but the deer. Tonight, I rest under the pines
and golden honey locusts, waiting.

Portrait of the Virus as Origin

The anniversary of this
unbearable blue:
this year, I spend it
the same way as last:
in the woods, amber
crunching under feet:
brown as my camouflage:
safe from possibility: last
year, it was not lonely
the way it is now: the wind:
only known by the season
between winter and spring lures
my sweater: the sun tempts me
into yellowing like a daffodil:
today, I will not light a candle
for this birthday: I will eat
a piece a cake: allow
the sugar to swell on my tongue.

Keeper

This city is littered with buildings built on hills—
here, companionships have become shallow boxes lined
with thin plywood to the hole's bottom dirt beneath—the stings
are what keep this from being simple, invisible welts
form with every new case. Tonight, on the fire escape,
sitting high above with the city below, I stare out into a field
of gently burning office buildings. Vacant and yet, still lit—
that yellow and white glimmer just before the candle's last stretch
of wick disappears. I can see into every window, a bee hive
of glowing squares—abandoned. The hum of wind hitting leaves
sings to me as I look down through the bars where I sit, wonder
how many bones will break if I fell. Wonder how much longer
I will be left here sitting safely, how many more swarms
will find homes in boxes with dirt beneath.

September's Start

I wish I found a willow
tree peering through my window,
swaddling my street,
embracing those walking
below, cradling those crying
as I am today, a hard day, a day
of moving.
     Instead, the window
of my new apartment watches
a decrepit corner liquor store
once belonging to Tom
in glaring Comic Sans.
I judge Tom only in his choice
of lettering. The building matches me—
exhausted wood pulling
from its paneling, broken
glass, peeling paint. I wonder
if Tom matches me too.

One Way High Way

What's your favorite time of day?

Before or after the accident?

After.

Night.

Why?

Because I can shut my eyes and see black, not red.

Were you present at the scene?

Yes, but I arrived late. Too late. All I saw was red everywhere, and I wasn't sure if the red was on the bodies and the pavement or if it was on the back of my eyelids. Everything seemed stained. Maybe it was paint. It could have been paint, right? I know she had been wearing a white shirt. I remember because I saw her right before she left and it looked great on her. Maybe because she was the epitome of the color. The shirt wasn't white anymore when I saw her after. I wanted to take off that shirt—see the pale of her body underneath. I wanted to toss it in the washing machine and wash out the paint.

Was it paint?

No.

How did you find out?

I touched her.

Where?

On her stomach, where the color was darkest—a lovely deep red. I would have loved to paint with it. But I don't think it would have been very tasteful. Well, then again, why not? She knew a lot of things I didn't know and will never know.

If There Ever Comes a Day

Pumpkin muffins pulled from the oven
just a few minutes early, sending sweetness to
retrieve me from my bedroom. Wooden brush
bristles running through strawberry
blond hair, feeding strand after strand
into a set of French braids. Our steps in unison
behind pawprints down the muddy back pathway
to school, lined with fences of honeysuckle and ivy.
Bare branches circling the lake through the window,
novels alongside fire crackling with anticipated flurries.
John Denver walking us through rain and calling us home.
A teary wave as the car drives away, unlike

so many times before. In my ear, I hear
you whisper: *it always hits the one that's left,*
not the one who leaves.

Portrait of the Virus as Epidermis

Facing him allows her to swallow
the pills. After, they are companions.

When she is prepared, she happily
becomes his host—welcoming his body

of wind into the hospital room, swiftly
serving him tea and blueberry macarons. Outside,

the breeze is cool—here, the warmth scurries
in circles like a dog chasing his tail. He pulls

at the dark underneath her skin, as routine
as the flow of blood. Each year he grows

heavier—like a prisoner, she continues
to carry him within her.

Namesake

In another life, I am her:
whiskey poured religiously—drowning
the clock's five chimes. A mind
decisive and driven, decorated
with a college degree, companionship
found in heeled clicks on firm floors—
devotion to remedy, loyalty. Two-bedroom
apartment—a spare for collected
coins, books of poetry, boxes
of handwriting on yellowed paper.
Eighty-seven years of
(if not strength) sanctuary
in solitude until breath
became both air and cloud.
But in this life, she sits poised
against my moss-green walls,
lips unmoving, face gentle, my same blue
eyes following as I rise each day
to take the complacent path she defied—
and the worst is, when I look in the mirror,
she no longer answers.

Sunset, Moonrise

God is perfected—stripped
of coverings, splashed with water,
and made new. Each drip,
a reminder of each child

coiled. The sun has nothing
to be happy about, the stars—
no sadness. Her body—limp, yet
clean. Plum trees grow in place

of these children, scattered about
Her body—purple crimson freckles.
She gives the fruit to the survivors—
an effort to keep the angels away.

They happily take each plump plum,
mash it into pulp, spread it swiftly
upon their breakfast bread before
going about their day. She watches

from above, tells the sun
it has something to be happy
about as it gives birth to the moon.

Passing Home

An endless lullaby—wind
rustling through leaves

leaving only a few survivors,
light pouring through the absences—

kaleidoscope of red, yellow, brown.
Looking up, my face is wet with those

left drifting. I needed
to help them, needed

to run back to my house—
feet scuffing their brothers and sisters—

rummage through the arts and crafts box,
to hurry back into the forest—

overflowing with shadows and eternal
trees—knowing a glue stick would fix it all.

Balance

It's September in Pennsylvania,
noon & I am in bed. The clouds guard
the sun like an overprotective brother.
The water is cold, the sun's lover in need of her
warm glow. These days my dog is my alarm, his mellow

whimpers pull my sight from black to light
& I know I must rise. In the kitchen, my feet
crack open the silence as I make coffee
with unfiltered water & filterless—
your disapproving eyes slice my back
with a butter knife, but you aren't here.

By the water's edge, I become a bird & perch
on the smallest rock. Under my weight, it tips.
The lake swallows my coffee. With the rhythm
of the waves, the ceramic fragments kiss the rock
below me. It makes me think of you.

Before Family Was But One

That morning, more of the same—sunrise, Cheerios and skim milk
poured until I said *when* from my father's hand, blackberries,
blueberries in a bowl on the table. Mondays and Wednesdays,
my mother would wake at four to swim, lap after lap. This was all before.

Before the landline call, before I knew a voice's crack, crack of metal.
Before I knew how my father looked when he cried—before bodies
on pavement, crimson stains, dusk calling to death. Before
I knew the chill of gray water, the sudden dimming of a lightbulb,

the loneliness of fresh carnations. Before I believed in God—after
is untouched black coffee on the counter.

Of Unbelonging

Leaves are like snowflakes—
I kill them under my weight,
feeling as close to God
as I ever have, teetering
with energy from the sun.
For each leaf, I create
a world, seek their mother tree.
Shriveled and curled, they find
a home wherever they land—
forgotten by us,
the most careless creatures.
In these woods, I am ruler,
a trespasser—the most unloved.
At the fork in the road,
I know either path I choose
will be the wrong one.

Portrait of the Virus as Clarity

It was the season of waiting—the moon
grew grayer, the sun dimmer

as if on a timer.   *Now*, it said.
          The world was no longer green,
nor golden. Only

a silence we could see,
but we stayed away. It was the figment who told us
                              God was sick—
She came to us in echoes, in sways

of naked branches—it was the first time
              we did not question.

We held our ears
to the dirt, listened for Her lessons.

              This was the moment we learned
about the creation of a shadow.

WINTER

Growing Grief

In the innermost pocket of Ben's wallet is a pinch of white fur, a piece of you he carries with him. It's there when he wanders down the cracker aisle of Whole Foods, when he orders a pistachio latte from Blank Street, when he unlocks his bike and starts his commute to work. It's there when he comes home to find me slouched on the couch, broken and alone.

Our new Boston apartment has big windows that look out over the river, a porch with furniture we picked out last summer, a dishwasher, even a roofdeck. Yesterday, it was perfect. Now the walls feel too white, the floor too slick, the space too big—it has everything but you.

A sliver of light peeks from behind the bedroom shades. It's 6am. Below me, your bed is filled with empty silence that shatters me. I pull the shades tighter shut, praising the darkness as it hugs around me. I take a deep breath. It makes me feel mostly dead.

This time last week, you sat beside me. Now, it's 1pm when I roll out of bed, leave a piece of uneaten toast on the counter, and realize nothing is okay. Ben suggests we leave—take a walk. We take the stairs, walk along the water, wander the Mall. There's a bench there with a bucket of treats beside it. We talk about you.

Ben says the sunset's not very good today, and we both know that nothing is good today. Nothing may ever be good again. You were the good, the sole reason I got out of bed, the why I worked hard at my job, the one thing I loved fully. Now you're the collar in my purse, the bowls in the living room, the plush red dinosaur under the coffee table, but you're not you. And you're not here. I was so lucky to love you.

We walk back into our building, take the stairs, and I put the keys in the knob, wishing so badly you will be there, by the door, waiting for me.

Figment

Last night, Blue Morpho butterflies escaped
my mouth when I tried to speak, fluttered
up and kissed my eyelashes—a dream.
You were there too—we were riding in a car,
windows down, breeze whipping through our hair.

Over the wind in my ears I heard you say
Last weekend, I almost hit a butterfly in this car—
it was raining. Thank God I didn't—its wings
so weighty with water, but its flicker still graceful.
I held my breath until I disappeared.

When I woke, I was in my childhood room.
There were bookshelves with photos of people
I no longer knew, pink, yellow, and blue butterflies
floating on the walls, shadows reflecting
off of them, onto the white curtains made

for me as a child. In the muted dark,
I connected your features, saw you emerging
from the linen in the half-light before wings appeared
and you followed the butterflies on the walls.

That Winter Felt Like Cutting into an Onion:

Painful in more ways than one.
I realized I had grown so very full
of tears, bullshit, empty promises,
sweets, ice cream, lemon cake, wine
that never fully had the effect I wish it did.
Perhaps even the opposite.
I knew I was going to burst,
eventually. Each week that winter, alone,
I grew older, the weather grew colder.
On Sundays, I would set out to buy
a new vice, a revised way to rot.
Over twelve Sundays, the days
grew longer. The rest of the world
set out in the sun, bathed in the light.
I remained plump and full,
with the ever present feeling
of onions in my eyes.

Barren City

He is trying to teach us—this Time
It is the capital H cast in the Sunbeams
That overflow my pane
In the Morning—scuff marks

On hardwood—specks in the Space
Between bricks in the sidewalk—
In the square where a brick had been—
Air that expands into each Corner

Of the room as soon as the cracked
Window whirls the Dust alive—grass
Billowing along the Charles—motionless
Ducks in the garden—my God, the bluejay

Blurting into Oblivion, to the oblivious—
Bees, ceasing, deceased—Red wine
In the fridge—the orchid wilting on
A sill in sunlight—obedient Dog
At the door—the shadow behind Him.

I took my love

and took it down the endless I-84 trek west to the lake. You pulled into the Dunkin parking lot. It was the week he died. I couldn't get out of the car—you brought me a nonfat caramel latte without my asking. Face wet, I queued songs that I knew would let me cry, not that it was a challenge then. I needed to bask in it. I described it to you as the heavy emptying, the deep of hopelessness, but you knew what I meant and how nothing could quite cover it. We started with Jewel's "You Were Meant For Me" then Fleetwood Mac's "Landslide." Your left hand held the wheel while your right held me. For the five hours, through towns and mountains, there I was—

head limp, my body
unmoving. Someone might have
thought I was dead too.

A Hike

Nobody on
the mountain,
my only companion
the white
beneath me,
and the evergreens
lining either side.
I perch at the top,
a queen overlooking
her subjects,
but unlike her
(or maybe like her),
my body breathes
with fear. The sea
of snow sways—
God's voice
creasing the air.
In the distance,
mountains multiply—
they are calla lilies
blind to the glacial
dark. Here the sun
and snow are lovers,
though only
until the green
of summer calls.

Claustrophilia

This window is painted with handprints
of someone I don't know, little smudges
that mimic me—a child's drawing
in crayon on the wall. I used to find

sanctuary looking out this glass and bathe
in the falling leaves. Now I see
dirty marks scraping,
screeching, clouding my view of the cows

and curving canals, the ghost
of who I thought I was. How to unfeel
the pooling of blood in feet,
the hoping to jolt

awake—sweaty, relieved.
I have never been as sad as I have been here,
I try to soothe the English sky as it sobs with me
most days. It locks me in the attic, burns

my skin, scars my flesh
like freckles. I have found a place can modify—
it twists, smothers, suffocates.
And when I leave, I pity the people

who stay and ask if it is the place
that I so dislike, or what happened
here. When I died—I fell
into the dull of a hole

and the mud piled upon me.
I liked the coolness, the escape
that required no effort. Mud filled
my mouth, that's when I could breathe.

Triggering Town

Here, the trees keep me company—
I reflect my life onto them, mimic
their mannerisms and branch my arms
to follow, but all the time I'm moving.
As I walk, I make sure to speak,
if only to the dog below me—it's winter
and I do not wish to be hunted.
With each step, I flirt with danger,
keeping my head up and my faux fur hood down.
Last week, driving to the cabin,
I passed a truck of chickens, packed like anchovies,
clucking too weakly to be heard
over the engines. Today, I am those chickens—
I pray the hunter above me will become a vegetarian.

Winter Meditation

Each day, the sun
setting leaves me
feeling weightless—
it takes my body,
slowly folding
from bright blue
to yellow into red.
The colors run
like blood
through veins
to an open wound.
With each second,
night grows heavier
until the comforter
is completely pulled
over the eyelid
of the earth.

Early January

For Ben

The moment of resolutions. It's decided—I'll read more
books. Now I sit in bed underneath the duvet, a plush
blanket wrapped around me, our only child—our puppy—at
my feet and a poem in my lap. You breathe steadily beside
me, newly asleep. I count your exhales and match mine
to yours—unison, I think. Together. In my cycle class, the
instructor preaches about getting my life together. To no
one in particular, he says, *this will be your year—your chance to
stop dating mediocre men, start loving yourself.* The words float
higher and higher into the exhausted room. I smile, slow my
legs—think of you. I've already won. My resolution:

Mirror the stars in
the way they devotedly
adore the full moon.

I-84 West is the Trailer for the Apocalypse:

paralyzed
black tar buries
the raw earth
like a deceased
friend. Boxes
of moving metal
exhale poison
as they cut
through forests,
fields, towns.
Possum, squirrel,
doe discarded
by rushing tires
carrying oblivious
spectators:
a grassless graveyard,
the aftermath
of a festival. Empty cans
and papers catch
and fall, decorating
the cool black
like colorful confetti.
Joyless drive:
o, stolen land.

SPRING

Room of the Hostage Heart

Covered only by an oak tree,
he found me crying on the lounge chair

out by the back creek. My hair had fallen
over my face—I didn't dare speak of the sadness.

For all season, I had been happily gone—
the distance between us stretching a silence,

ruthless, thick. I pretended I was not there,
but the weight of my body illuminated my skin.

Looking the stillness in the face, I said
it was about a boy, an end to my age

of infatuation, a ripe fruit cleaved. It was his arms
that answered, like the faint halo of the sun

behind the clouds. I should have known
he knew, for he had lived a life before.

Long Distance Lover

The sun carries my messages
to him 8138 miles away:
when I dog-ear the page
of my book and pull
down the covers to mark the end

of my day, he wakes.
I'd say we are like ships
passing in the night,
the miles like buckets
of water between us,

but that would be unbearably clichéd.
Each morning I greet the sun
like I would greet him
if he were here. I peek open
the curtains and smile. I say

"good morning, sun."
Unlike he would, she doesn't reply.
I don't take it personally,
I continue the ritual—
I know she and the moon

are the only things
that connect our immense distance.
On FaceTime, he told me
his coworker thought
it was absurd that Americans

don't eat rice at every meal.
I said I thought the idea
of eating rice at every meal
was absurd. He said

he was stuck in the middle.
It's not a bad place to be,
but the thing is,
it's without me.

Lessons

After "Time of Need" by Allison Seay

From the rubbing of spade on skin,
my hands bleed, deep red

runs onto the flesh
of the Earth. Alongside me, among

the English daisies and dirt,
my Sister works silently—

first year of many—she and I,
together, digging, sharing

space—we learn the seasons this way,
and I don't mind her steady glances

throughout the day to see
if I am still beside her.

Lips

1.

Kissing a girl, and wondering why you did it. Did you like it? Kissing a boy and feeling closer to your faith, but remembering not to kiss too many. Kissing a Cavalier King Charles Spaniel, but not your Cavalier King Charles Spaniel. Would your dog think that was cheating?

2.

Expressing your love, not too quickly though. Play some games first. Everyone loves (a) Monopoly. Expressing your hatred, or maybe just the neutral numbness that your hatred produces when marinated in ginger and brown sugar. Both seem to free you from the snarl of your stomach.

3.

Bashing your enemies. Dig underneath the(ir) graves, extract the wet earth. Use this soil to plant a new succulent for your living room. Bashing your friends, or are your friends actually your enemies? Human bodies are not transparent.

4.

Articulating your emotions. Not articulating your emotions. Talk to your sister, I'm sure she's mastered this one by now and would love to teach you. After, tell her she gets her charm from your mother.

5.

Leading others to your ideas. Or better yet, confusing others and then ignoring them. I heard that was a very effective tactic if you're looking to hurt the people you care about. Hurting the people you don't care about. Enjoying it. You more than likely carry this (s)kill like a mint on the tip of your tongue.

Closet of Overflowing Apologies

Today is a day
gray from clouds
to pavement—
the bees releasing
their stingers mark
the descension:
this is the rainy
season, the field of call
without response, era
of crumpled cans
confetting the sidewalk,
session of starvation, term
of pollenness suffocation,
the long calendar
of laying, time
of littered window
boxes, season of
disregard for you.

Gentle Echo

In the grass, I lay face up, on
the blue patterned tapestry

you bought for me in Monterosso,
eyes shut to keep from being stained

with light, limbs level
with contentment, mind heavy

with memory—that starlit night,
half-empty bottle of red pressed to my lips,

together overlooking the lit windows of Manarola.
And suddenly you stomp on my chest, two feet

first in unison—rising, falling of color and beat—
then more softly as the day goes on,

as if your body has grown tired
(as mine has) but your spirit has not.

Matter of Vision

The breeze is hitting on my shoulders,
tapping to ask if I would like
to join him. The way there so dark
and narrow, clouded
with shadows and blae-colored bricks—
I find my worth slipping
through my fingers, puddling below

and I ask myself why he's always here,
every time, it is the same.
He's in the smell of apple soap
in the morning, in the pistol aimed
at my own dog, in the sizzling cigarette
ashes falling from the floor above. I ask
why it all sounds so good late at night,
when I'm curled in my bed, alone

letting my hair flow, trying to rein
in my thoughts of jealousy
and possibility. But when
the sun again haunts
my window, it will finally be light
enough to see his flaws, my flaws,
the other that is outside of us.
The breathing above me, as the sheets
billow around, again
pulls at my skin
and carries my mind away
with him.

Love Note

For my mother, After "Aquarium" by Audrey Dubois

You sit in the corner
of the bookstore (your favorite)
as your mother reads—
not looking onto the book,
but to her. Her stillness
is genuine, unfamiliar—
no longer the fast frantic
of a mother who has provided
for four other humans. She reminds
you of an evergreen amaryllis,
the moment between when the hygienist
leaves the room and the dentist walks in,
the color yellow, the crack of a freshly
printed paperback, the transition from bold
flame to steady flicker of a freshly lit candle,
the fizz of champagne, the smell that accompanies
the anticipation of snow: the spring that follows.

Next Talking Point

In between sips of bloody mary,
a near stranger asks me:
what's your earliest memory?
When all I hear is ringing,
I give up on the idea
that it has to be my earliest,

and see myself crouching behind
the yellow and blue gingham plush chair
in the living room, or caressing
the head of the black stone dog
in front of where the dining room walls kiss,
or my hand in the secret hiding place
in the rip of my grandfather's
orange recliner.

I turn back to the stranger.
She has moved on to the next
interesting thing, and I realize
you can make a tomato into anything
but you can't make any thing into a tomato.

Together in the Grass

We were at a party, surrounded
by the soft opening of spring,

when he first whispered he loved me:
in memory, night reflected in his eyes—navy

of a koi pond, freckles floating like flurries
through his irises. Behind us, noise,

shimmers that stain even the insides
of eyelids, the amplified clink of bottles.

He first tried to say it here, but I turned
my back to keep from being blinded,

from going deaf. The next day, we sat
together in the grass, in the rain.

He remembered to bring an umbrella
of silence. I wished I had brought a book.

Daylight Saving

The sunlight explores the walls
of the apartment we share
like a rabid cockroach.
I crack the body
with a firm stomp, one foot—
shoeless. Together, the dog
I call the love of my life
and I hold a small service.

The dog has a few nice
things to say. I cry for the third
time today. The body lays
in a planter on the fire escape,
three inches down in the dirt,
where a month later grows
a peony, my favorite flower,
clearly in love with the light.

SUMMER

Last Night I Dreamed They All Blamed Me

My grandfather, laying,
humming like a low branch
in early wind. Together, the morning
sun and I pay a visit to his room.
It smells of a bamboo forest, I embrace
the oxygen.
                His sheets blizzard—
even in the storm, he finds my hand.
I ask him how he's doing.
It is deep summer, the fever month,
the fallen season, but still the linen
of his shirt, like him, is unwrinkled,
pristine. Against the near window,
the wind brushes a chrysanthemum
in bloom. If I were French,
I would have known. He replies
better now with a squeeze.

High School Love Story

You do not live as I do:
spinning on the top
step of the staircase,
leaning out the window,
the end of the line. Listen:
this life is cool like whipped cream
atop pie. Absolute like a lost leaf
in a garden. Its end is unbelonging
like words of poetry in your mouth,
truthful like the shadow of a rock
in the forest behind your house.
It's understanding, a lone weed
in a field of poppies. You stay
on the bottom step.

For the Love of Mothers

The world will always need more salt,
and light, and how-to productions

in the basement bathroom at the late hour
of 11, flutter of lips over lattes

at the coffee shop on Main, lunchbox
Post-it notes sending love and wishing

luck, hugs that follow the sting
of bra-stuffing swings flung

like serpents during school,
sharing the trick of bobby pins

as keys and safety pins as almost
anything—because there's no deeper

secret than the one found in the freshly
cut flowers on the bathroom counter.

Portrait of The Virus as Sovereign

The voice always begins as a whisper. Blurred
like the air that swirls through the room
as it brushes skeleton white curtains, rides
up walls, floats through hospital sheets.
It delivers bad news with pleasure.
The fever hits harder, the voice follows suit—

it no longer belongs to the nurses or doctors.
It grips at the throat, feeds on dread,
pulls me to follow—each day I grow closer.
The volume bounces among the stars
behind my eyelids, controls my shiver and chill.
My body is a city, the voice wants to be Queen.

Late Summer

Here, I've learned peace.
Cobwebs connecting branches

to trunks, shrubs that stare back,
watch as we walk, comfortable silence.

Green towers above—ensures I stay clean
as she, the woman who taught me love.

If only my body were a drop of water. The whistle
of the train by the James releases oxygen

from my lungs. With each tug, a memory of her:
hearing infant cries, she rose in the cold hours

of morning, the dark sky only beginning to rouse.
A symphony of weight on tracks travelled through

trees to reach two shadows keeping company.

Habitat

I welcome the summer
heat that leads to my fifth-floor
flat that smells like the edge
of a lake—perfume
of my childhood.
Time has committed
its favorite crime—
we no longer create
restaurants in the woods, plates
full with moss and twigs; the view
of the shore has changed,
the bones of the house torn
down and rebuilt.
My grandparents' hair
has grown too gray to visit
the rock-littered cottage.
In my flat, I heave
the windows open, bathe
in the harsh heat,
plaster this passing scent
onto my skin—pray it lasts.

August

Soon nature will become new, washed
of any lingering remnants of regret
from the summer, spring, winter.

I'll witness it from my window,
watch as the crisp cold kills
more than just weeds. I'll think of how,

at the end of our practice,
my yoga instructor will say the fetal
position is the representation

of rebirth, and I'll spend
the rest of the day
thinking about my previous deaths—

about how when the sun sets,
the light still remains, victorious.

Distance

Standing above me, her victim,
she told me: It was there
[I learned there is violence
in the whistle of the wind
through the open window,
weight of clouds mimicking
the weight of human breath]
in beauty school, I [found
solid glass beneath my feet,
enough time away from him
for my shoulders to unclench]
learned [to manipulate the strands,
control, shape—that's when
I finally knew how it felt to be him].

Temple

The world outside sways in color,
watching from above—

the steeple. Sweetgum leaves stretching
toward the Mother Sun, never satisfied,

undisturbed by the honking, exhaust,
nosy people. They don't know

they'll never be taller than the buildings
surrounding them—they keep trying.

Each window across the street is a portal
to another life. One: wasted food sitting

in the sink kept company by bowls, knives,
spoons, covered in forgotten streaks. Two:

face glowing before a screen, half-empty
wine glass in hand. Three: clouds

paying visit to the barred fire escape,
bringing rain, bringing light,

and my top-floor apartment
becomes just another pew.

It's July

After "It's July, So Let's" by Elise Powers

and I'm new to the city, unseasonably sun-soaked
and sweating, smaller with every step between glass
buildings that welcome me with "mind the queue"
and "mind the gap" and "you alright?"
How wonderfully wild it is that I am here,
supporting myself in this foreign place, across an ocean
from home. I will tell my future daughter: I dreamed
along the Thames when I was young, wrote poetry
under the willows in Camden. I plucked spines off shelves
of bookshops in Marylebone, ran my dog through Hyde Park
like I had nowhere better to be (and I didn't). I breathed
my version of life into a city I once had never known,
wrinkled my life into something well-worn,
well-loved, something worth risking for.

NOTES

"Triggering Town" borrows its title from Richard Hugo's book of essays entitled *The Triggering Town*.

"If There Ever Comes a Day" is a phrase borrowed from the following Winnie the Pooh quote: "If there ever comes a day when we can't be together, keep me in your heart, I'll stay there forever."

"Sunset, Moonrise" draws inspiration from Sylvia Plath's "Edge," published in her collection *Ariel*.

"I took my love" borrows its title from the 1975 Fleetwood Mac song "Landslide," reading "I took my love, I took it down / climbed a mountain and I turned around / and I saw my reflection in the snow covered hills / 'til the landslide brought me down."

"Love Note" is in direct response to Audrey Dubois' poem "Aquarium" published in Funicular Magazine in July 2021.

"Lessons" draws inspiration from "Time of Need" by Allison Seay, published in her collection *To See the Queen*.

"It's July" draws inspiration and borrows a phrase from "It's July, So Let's" by Elise Powers.

ACKNOWLEDGMENTS

I am deeply grateful to the following publications in which these individual poems, sometimes in previous drafts or with different titles, first appeared:

And So Yeah: "One Way High Way," "Claustrophilia," and "Lips"
Autofocus: "Balance"
Book + Bottle: "Love Note"
The Bookends Review: "Daylight Saving"
Bread & Butter: "Early January"
Chariot Press: "Last Night I Dreamed They All Blamed Me"
Dialogist Journal : "Season of Waiting"
The Elevation Review: "Portrait of the Virus as Clarity"
Eunoia Review: "Growing Grief" and "August"
Ghost City Review: "Barren City"
North Dakota Quarterly: "September's Start"
Poet Lore: "Portrait of the Virus as Origin"
Rock & Sling: "Before Family Was But One"
Up North Lit: "Room of the Hostage Heart"
West Trade Review: "Closet of Overflowing Apologies"
Yes Poetry: "Passing Home"

I am so incredibly grateful to Cornerstone Press at the University of Wisconsin–Stevens Point and the wonderful team who brought this book to life: Dr. Ross Tangedal, Brianna Loving, Allison Lange, Sophie McPherson, and Sam Bjork. Thank you for your guidance, dedication, and kindness throughout this process. I'd also like to express my deepest thanks to my talented friend Christa MacDonald who so artfully designed the cover of this collection, including one notable image taken by videographer and photographer (and my dear friend) Beth Pezzoni.

Additionally, thank you to my gifted teachers and mentors throughout the years: Lisa Winn, Pete Follansbee, Allison Seay, Brian Henry, Peter Lurie, Dan Tobin, and Steve Yarbrough. I think about the lessons I have learned from you—in writing and in life—often.

I'm also immensely grateful to and for my workshop cohort Livia Meneghin, Audrey Dubois, and Kate Kobosko—my best editor, faithful literary confidant, and true friend. Here's to endless discussions about both literature and life. You inspire me. Someday our own collections will be the book club picks of aspiring writers.

Thank you also to my beloved mom and dad for bringing me into this wild world, teaching me both beautiful and difficult lessons, and most importantly, always supporting me in my poetic endeavors. I realize now what a gift it is to grow up surrounded by people who encourage you to chase your dreams. And to my siblings: Kyle, Elliott, and Holly—I wouldn't be where I am today without your guidance, support, or love. I'm so lucky to have you in my corner, and am so grateful for all three of you.

To my Ben—thank you for reminding me that life is worth laughing at, and for being my biggest supporter, best friend, and forever partner. Because of you, when I feel joy, I don't hesitate. I know unconditional and undying love everyday because of you, Dusty, and Jerry. Lastly, to my people, your gestures of care and encouragement don't go unnoticed or unappreciated. Each one of you has changed my life in more ways than you realize. You may even be the inspiration for a poem in this book. Thank you.

KAKIE PATE has an MFA in Poetry from Emerson College in Boston, Massachusetts. Her poems have appeared in such journals as *Poet Lore, North Dakota Quarterly, Dialogist Journal, Rock & Sling,* and *Eunoia Review.* She worked for *Redivider* as the Head Poetry Editor and *Autofocus* as Social Media Manager. She grew up in Richmond, Virginia and now lives in London, England.